THE VIETNAM WAR
Lost Words

JEREMY SMITH

Copyright © ticktock Entertainment Ltd 2005
First published in Great Britain in 2005 by ticktock Media Ltd.,
Unit 2, Orchard Business Centre, North Farm Road, Tunbridge Wells, Kent, TN2 3XF
ISBN 1 86007 833 8 pbk
Printed in China
A CIP catalogue record for this book is available from the British Library.

CONTENTS

INTRODUCTION

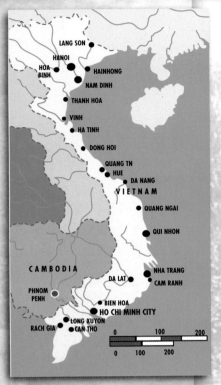

Above The country of Vietnam lies in South-east Asia. In the late 19th-early 20th century, Vietnam was occupied by the French and then the Japanese, before the Americans took over the mantle in 1954. The major battles of the Vietnam war are marked on the top map.

The Vietnam war was the most unpopular war the United States has ever fought in, and the only war it has ever lost. Almost 60,000 Americans lost their lives in the jungles of Vietnam while millions of Vietnamese from both sides perished. The cost of the war ran into hundreds of billions of dollars for the United States, and crippled the Vietnamese economy. Politically, events in Indochina have coloured American foreign policy ever since, while Vietnam has become isolated internationally. Today, decades later, the event still looms large in many people's lives in the United States, Vietnam, and around the world.

The crisis in Vietnam erupted during the 1940s, when large numbers of Vietnamese rose up against their French rulers. Chaos in Vietnam was temporarily resolved by a conference held in Geneva in 1954, which divided the country into a communist North and a democratic South. This division was only intended to be temporary, but because of political tensions elections to reunify Vietnam were never held, and many people in the West feared for the future of South Vietnam.

In the United States, president after president decided that South Vietnam must not be allowed to fall under the control of the Northern communists, and from 1954, an American presence was established in the country. At first, Americans were there only as advisors, training South Vietnamese troops to defend themselves from attack, but by 1965 they had become embroiled in a bitter military conflict that would last another eight years. In the process, almost 60,000 American servicemen were killed in the jungles of Vietnam, together with more than a million Vietnamese. In 1973, swayed by rising revulsion at the war from their public, and a realisation that this conflict in the jungles of South-east Asia could not be won, American politicians decided that South Vietnam would have to stand alone. Just two years after American troops left the country, troops and tanks from Hanoi in the North rumbled into Saigon and Le Duan declared the birth of a communist Republic of Vietnam. The nightmare for the United States had come true, as soon afterwards, the neighbouring countries of Laos and Cambodia both turned communist.

Peace for Vietnam proved to be short-lived, however. The country was at conflict again almost immediately, after it made the decision

Above *The jungles of Vietnam were a terrain alien to most American soldiers.*

Left *United States troops were ill-equipped to fight a war in the jungles of Vietnam.*

Above *South Vietnamese troops try to defend their capital, Saigon, from attack. By 1973, their battle was becoming increasingly desperate.*

to invade Cambodia in 1978 and install a pro-Vietnamese party in power. The following year, Vietnam was at war with China, backed by the United States. These wars, together with the damage caused during the war with United States, mean that even today, Vietnam is one of the poorest countries in the world. The damage to the prestige of the United States that resulted from its defeat on the battlefield was immense. American administrations retaliated by freezing all trade and diplomatic relations between the two countries. The United States also aired its grievances on an international stage, blocking Vietnam's entry into the United Nations. Soldiers returning home from the war also faced serious problems. They were vilified by some members of the public for what they had believed was "doing their duty", many found it difficult to settle back into civilian life. Abused and discriminated against, many resorted to drink and drugs to ease the pain. Internationally, defeat in Vietnam may have made the United States more cautious about committing troops to conflicts, and the next major battle was not until the 1991 Gulf War.

Today, the scars of the war in Vietnam are beginning to fade. As the Cold War gradually became a

Left *Vietnam was a poor country based on traditional farming methods when the war began. Here two girls are farming a rice paddy.*

conflict of the past with the collapse of the USSR and the Eastern Bloc, people began to think about reconciliation. President Clinton began the process of restoring relations between the two countries in 1994, and today, many hundreds of thousands of Americans visit Vietnam every year as tourists. Many Vietnamese people who emigrated to America have brought up a generation of children in the United States. These Amerasian children stand as a living bond between the two countries. Back in Vietnam, too, thousands of children were born as a result of relationships between American soldiers and South Vietnamese women. However, problems caused by the war remain. Vietnam remains desperately poor, and citizens from the South who fought against the communists continue to suffer discrimination. In the United States, around a quarter of all homeless people in the United States are Vietnam veterans, while families from both sides who lost loved ones during the conflict continue to grieve, and will never forget their loss.

Above Street traders in Hanoi, Vietnam, sell their wares to tourists from all over the world, including the United States. This colourful garland is decorated in the colours of the Vietnamese flag.

Left President Bill Clinton was in part responsible for the improving relations between Vietnam and the United States. Here, Bill Clinton is shown with Vietnam's Prime Minister Phan Van Khai in a conference in Auckland, New Zealand in 1998.

Above In America, anti-communist propaganda appeared on bubble-gum cards like the one above. Ho Chi Minh was portrayed as an evil man with a twisting, snarling face.

For many centuries Vietnam has had a tradition of rejecting foreign interference in their affairs. First conquered by the Chinese in 111 BC, the people of Vietnam mounted several unsuccessful rebellions until in 938 AD they regained their independence. A further brief period of Chinese rule in the 15th century failed to suppress the proud Vietnamese identity, and the country expanded its territory until Europeans arrived in the region in the 19th century.

Right Dr. Ho Chi Minh, President of Vietnam and the leader of their fight for independence, accepts ovations from the public during a visit to Delhi, 1958.

"All men are created equal. They are endowed by their Creator with certain inalienable rights; among these are life, liberty and the pursuit of happiness. Those are undeniable truths... The French have fled, the Japanese have capitulated, Emperor Bao Dai has abdicated. Our people have broken the chains which for nearly a century have fettered us, and have won independence for the Fatherland. The whole Vietnamese people, animated by a common purpose, are determined to fight to the bitter end against any attempt by the French colonialists to re-conquer our country. We are convinced that the Allied nations, led by America, Britain and the Soviet Union have acknowledged the principles of self-determination and the equality of nations... and will not refuse to acknowledge the independence of Vietnam... The entire Vietnamese people are determined to mobilise all their physical and mental strength, to sacrifice their lives and property, in order to safeguard their independence and freedom."

Ho Chi Minh, declaring the independence of the Democratic Republic of Vietnam, September 2, 1945.

> "Vietnam must have a communist party... so the peasantry will overthrow the French Imperialists, seize political power, and set up the dictatorship of peasants and workers in order to achieve a communist society ."
>
> *Ho Chi Minh "The Communists Must Organize Themselves into a Single Party," 1929*
>
> "First, you must understand that to gain independence from a great power like France is a formidable task that cannot be achieved without some outside help... One must gain it through organization, propaganda, training and discipline."
>
> *Ho Chi Minh to U.S. intelligence officer Charles Fenn, 1945*

TIMELINE
111 BC-1930

111 BC
Kingdom of Vietnam conquered by Chinese.

939 AD
Vietnamese people end Chinese rule.

1407-1428
Further brief period of Chinese rule in Vietnam.

1858
France attacks Vietnam and occupies Saigon.

FEB, 1930
Vietnamese Communist party formed by Ho Chi Minh.

FRENCH CONQUERORS

After repeated attempts, France finally gained control of Vietnam, Cambodia and Laos (as French Indo-China) by 1887. The French built railways and roads, hospitals and schools, mainly in South Vietnam. It was not until the 1930s that an organised Vietnamese resistance to French control began to emerge. In 1929, the communist Ho Chi Minh (born Nguyen That Thanh) set up the Indo-chinese Communist Party (ICP) in Hong Kong. In 1940, a Franco-Japanese agreement allowed Japan to occupy Vietnam during World War II. Ho Chi Minh returned to Vietnam in 1941, set up the Vietminh nationalist organisation, and called for an uprising against the country's foreign rulers. This revolt forced the Vietnamese-born, but Japanese-controlled Emperor Bao Dai to abdicate. When Japan surrendered to the Allies on September 2, 1945, Ho proclaimed the birth of the Democratic Republic of Vietnam. Any prospect of peaceful transition was soon dashed. In the aftermath of an

Below *A French sergeant inspects his troops in Vietnam, 1950.*

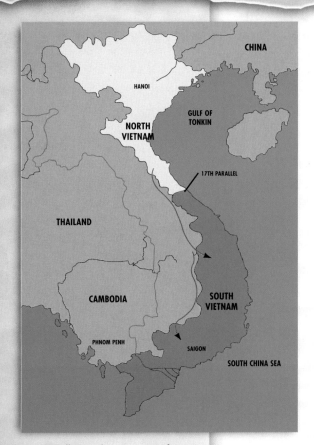

Above *Following the Geneva Conference, Vietnam was divided into North and South at the 17th Parallel, a line referred to as the demilitarized zone (DMZ).*

Right *The French presence in Vietnam was bitterly resented by much of the Vietnamese population.*

Allied victory in World War II, Great Britain and China were given the task of accepting the Japanese surrender in Vietnam. Chinese troops moved into North Vietnam and British troops, supporting the French desire to take back control of Vietnam, arrived in the South. There, they joined with French forces to drive Ho's forces out of Saigon. While British and Chinese forces left Vietnam in 1946, the French stayed. They persuaded Bao Dai to return as leader of Vietnam, and between 1946 and 1954, French troops fought a vicious battle with the Vietminh for control of the country. In 1945, President Roosevelt was opposed to French claims in Vietnam, but by the end of the decade the new climate of the Cold War meant that the United States placed its support behind French efforts to drive out the Vietminh. Increasingly concerned about the spread of communism across the world (a fear that escalated when China and much of eastern Europe turned communist), and believing that Ho Chi Minh was controlled by the USSR, America began to view the future of Vietnam as critical. When Eisenhower's refusal to support the French led to their defeat at Dienbienphu in 1954, the United States realised they might have to become more directly involved in Vietnam if they were to prevent it turning communist.

THE GENEVA CONFERENCE

While the French were suffering defeat in Vietnam, a conference was being held in Geneva to try to determine the future of the country. On July 21 a cease-fire was signed, which temporarily divided the country into North and South. It was also agreed that elections would be held in the country within two years, with a view to reunifying the country. Under the terms of the agreement, Ho Chi Minh formed a government in the North, while the stocky, chain-smoking Ngo Dinh Diem was made South Vietnam's Prime Minister in June 1954. Diem did not want elections to

"You have a row of dominoes set up; you knock over the first one, and what will happen to the last one is that it will go over very quickly... Asia, after all, has already lost some 450 million of its peoples to the Communist dictatorship, and we simply can't afford greater losses... But when we come to the possible sequence of events, the loss of Indo-china, of Burma, of Thailand, of the Peninsula, and Indonesia following, now you begin to talk about areas that not only multiply the disadvantages that you would suffer through the loss of materials, sources of materials, but now you are talking about millions and millions of people. Finally, the geographical position achieved thereby does many things. It turns the so-called island defensive chain of Japan, Formosa, of the Philippines and to the southward; it moves in to threaten Australia and New Zealand. It takes away, in its economic aspects, that region that Japan must have as a trading area or Japan, in turn, will have only one place in the world to go--that is, toward the Communist areas in order to live...So, the possible consequences of the loss are just incalculable to the free world."

President Eisenhower's "Domino Theory" speech, Presidential Press Conference April 7, 1954.

Below *An ARVN Radio Operator, pictured in 1958.*

be held, because he believed that Ho would win easily. He turned away from the French and towards the Americans for support and reassurance. The formation of the South East Asia Treaty Organisation (SEATO), in which the United States and a number of other countries agreed to protect South Vietnam from aggression, marked the beginning of a deepening American involvement in the country.

TOWARDS CIVIL WAR

As it became obvious that elections to unify the two countries would never be held, the United States became determined to support Diem's government. By 1958 it had invested more than a billion dollars in the regime. Ngo Dinh Diem's Army of the Republic of Vietnam (ARVN) waged a brutal war on communists based in the south. In response, Ho Chi Minh's government in Hanoi decided it was time to strike back. Members of Ho's North Vietnamese Army (NVA) were sent into South Vietnam by a route through Cambodia and Laos known as the Ho Chi Minh trail. In 1960, communist supporters in the South formed the National Liberation Front (NLF), referred to by Diem as the Viet Cong, to organize resistance efforts. The People's Liberation Armed Forces (PLAF)

TIMELINE 1941-1960

MAY, 1941
Ho Chi Minh helps to form the Vietminh organization.

MARCH, 1945
Japanese-French government appoint Emperor Bao Dai head of Vietnam.

SEPT 2, 1946
Ho Chi Minh declares Vietnamese independence.

MAY 7, 1954
Vietminh defeat the French at Dienbienphu.

JULY 21, 1954
Geneva Accords temporarily divides Vietnam in two.

OCT 26, 1955
Diem elected President of South Vietnam.

DEC 20, 1960
National Liberation Front (NLF) formed in South.

"I would like to be able to report... I saw all the signs of misery and oppression that have made my visits to East Germany like nightmare journeys to 1984. But it was not so. At first it was difficult for me, as it is for any Westerner, to conceive of a Communist government's genuinely 'serving the people'. I could hardly imagine a Communist government that was also a popular government... But this is just the sort of government the palm-hut state actually was while the struggle with the French continued. The Vietminh could not possibly have carried on the resistance for one year, let alone nine years, without the people's strong, united support."

American Joseph Alsop's report for the New Yorker, 1955.

Above *South Vietnamese service medal awarded to foreign soldiers who served in the country after 1960.*

Below *An American army chief instructs South Vietnamese soldiers about boarding procedures for an airlift on the US Army helicopter.*

"Five or six Viet Cong guys stopped my bus one morning to check the identity cards of the passengers. They dragged two men off the bus, and their chief said to them: 'We've been waiting for you. We've warned you many times to leave your jobs but you haven't obeyed. So now we must carry out the sentence.'

"They forced the two men to kneel by the roadside and one of the Viet Cong guys chopped off their heads with a machete. They then pinned verdicts to their shirts saying that the murdered men were policemen. The verdicts had been written out beforehand. It was horrible to watch."

Bus driver from Long Khanh province, northeast of Saigon, 1959.

was formed to run the military side. Viet Cong members attempted to convert South Vietnamese citizens to their cause using a mixture of assistance and intimidation, with brutal attacks carried out on citizens who were suspected of colluding with the government and the United States.

AMERICAN ASSISTANCE

In 1961, when John F Kennedy took office as President of the United States, American aid to South Vietnam reached an unprecedented level. President Kennedy's commitment to Vietnam as a vital Cold War battleground was crystallized when he told a reporter from The New York Times, "Now we have a problem in making our power credible, and Vietnam is the place." Special Forces called Green Berets were sent to Vietnam to train Diem's North Vietnamese ARVN in guerrilla warfare, a type of fighting more suited to the jungles of Vietnam. Civilian Irregular Defence Groups (CIDGs) were established to provide surveillance in the mountains, while 2,600 settlements known as "strategic

"I joined the anti-colonial underground when I was in my teens. I needed an occupation so I could live unnoticed in the South. I decided to open a noodle soup shop. It would be a great place to shelter revolutionaries on the run...

Most of my customers were US diplomats, military brass and soldiers. I'd be smiling and serving soup to the Americans downstairs while the high command upstairs was planning their victory over the United States."

Viet Cong spy Toai, speaking in 1991.

"We are launched on a course from which there is no respectable turning back: the overthrow of the Diem government. There is no turning back because US prestige is already publicly committed to this end in large measure, and will become more so as the facts leak out. In a more fundamental sense, there is no turning back because there is no possibility, in my view, that the war can be won under a Diem administration."

Henry Cabot Lodge, August 29, 1963.

TIMELINE
1962-1963

FEB, 1962
Military Assistance Command Vietnam (MACV) established by America to support South Vietnam.

MAY-AUG, 1963
Diem faces angry protests by Buddhists, after his police raid a pagoda claiming it was sheltering communists.

NOV 3, 1963
Kennedy does not intervene and Diem is assassinated.

NOV 22, 1963
Kennedy assassinated.

hamlets" were placed under the watch of armed guards. At the same time the number of American advisors in Vietnam soared from fewer than 1,000 in 1961 to more than 12,000 by the following year.

THE END OF DIEM

American plans to protect South Vietnam were further complicated by the fact that Diem was becoming increasingly unpopular with his own people. Diem, a Catholic, found his relations with the country's Buddhist majority increasingly strained, and when he enforced a rule banning the display of religious flags during a Buddhist festival, Buddhists in Hue took to the streets. Diem's troops responded by opening fire on the demonstrators. In response, a monk called Thich Quang Duc set fire to himself, grabbing headlines across the world. When news reached America that a coup was planned for November 1, Kennedy – realising that Diem was not the man to bring stability to Vietnam – decided not to intervene to protect him. On November 2, Diem and his brother Ngo Dinh Nhu were murdered by ARVN soldiers. Ironically, Kennedy was also assassinated less than three weeks later, and the Vietnam question passed to Vice President Lyndon B Johnson.

Below *South Vietnamese soldiers wade into a canal to lure Viet Cong guerrillas from flooded paddy fields.*

CHAPTER 2

BUILD UP A DEVELOPING CRISIS

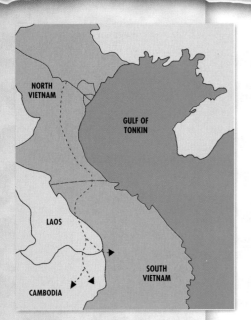

Above *A map showing the Gulf of Tonkin, scene of the incident that sparked the escalation of the Vietnam conflict. The arrows show the route south used by North Vietnamese troops.*

Below *President Lyndon B Johnson pins medals on US troops in recognition of deeds performed in battle in Vietnam.*

With the assassination of Diem and President Kennedy, civil unrest in South Vietnam, and a growing determination in the North to exploit this weakness, the prospect of a large-scale conflict in Vietnam had never been greater. Within just three years, the possibility of stationing American forces in South Vietnam had become a reality.

THE GULF OF TONKIN INCIDENT

After the death of Diem, power in South Vietnam was passed between several figures who seemed unable to restore order. The situation was made even more critical because from December 1963 large numbers of troops were being sent South by Ho Chi Minh. To many Americans, it seemed that the South Vietnamese were unable or unwilling to fight this threat, and it became increasingly clear to the new President, Lyndon B Johnson, that America might have to commit more directly to the fight in Vietnam. He would need to find the justification for escalating the conflict, however, and such an opportunity presented itself in the summer of 1964. On August 2, North Vietnamese gunboats attacked the American ship the *Maddox*, employed on a spying mission off the coast of North Vietnam, an attack that was recorded by photographers. Two days later, the *Maddox* and another American boat, the *Turner Joy* reported that they had been attacked during the night. There was no physical evidence of this attack, however, and many people (including the North Vietnamese authorities and several US senators) claim that it never took place.

"As far as we can see there are only three North Vietnamese boats, but we're having trouble with illumination…"

Telephone call from Admiral US Grant Sharp, commander of the Pacific Fleet, to Air Force General David Burchinal of the Joint Chiefs of Staff, August 4, 1964.

"To this day I don't know what happened… in the Tonkin Gulf… I think we may have made two serious misjudgements."

Former Defense Secretary Robert McNamara speaking to General Giap in Hanoi, November 1995.

Above *President Johnson authorised a massive bombing campaign in North Vietnam.*

DEC, 1963
NVA units head south into South Vietnam.

JUNE 20, 1964
General Westmoreland becomes head of MACV.

AUG 2, 1964
North Vietnamese attack on US ship *Maddox*. Reports of a further attack on the *Maddox* and another ship, the *Turner Joy*, leads to proposal and passing of Gulf of Tonkin resolution.

FEB 7, 1965
NLF attacks US military base in Pleiku.

FEB 13, 1965
President Johnson orders Operation Rolling Thunder.

FEB 8, 1965
First US troops land in Vietnam.

After receiving the reports from the two American boats, President Johnson asked Congress to support retaliatory strikes. On the basis of the information that was presented to them, Congress passed overwhelmingly a plan of action called the Gulf of Tonkin Resolution, which gave Johnson the power to go to war in Vietnam. When Viet Cong forces attacked and damaged an American air base near Saigon, American warplanes began bombing North Vietnam. Polls suggested that this action was backed by most of the American public.

GETTING IN DEEP

In February 1965, Viet Cong forces attacked an American camp near Pleiku, killing eight soldiers and wounding more than 100 others. A massive wave of air attacks on North Vietnam, known as Rolling Thunder, was unleashed in retaliation. In the following spring, Johnson sent huge

"North Vietnamese naval units… in violation of international law, have deliberately and repeatedly attacked United States naval vessels… The United States regards as vital to its national interest and to world peace the maintenance of international peace and security in South East Asia. Consonant with the Constitution of the United States and the Charter of the United Nations and in accordance with its obligations under the South East Asia Collective Defence Treaty, the United States is therefore prepared, as the President determines, to take all necessary steps, including the use of armed force, to assist any member or protocol state of the South East Asia Collective Defense Treaty requesting assistance in defence of its freedom."

The Gulf of Tonkin Resolution, August 1964.

Above *The logo of the United States Marine Corps.*

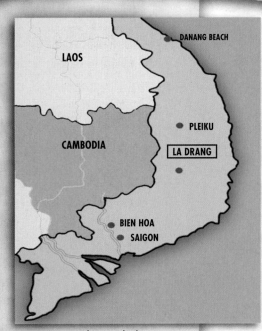

LAOS
CAMBODIA
DANANG BEACH
PLEIKU
LA DRANG
BIEN HOA
SAIGON

Above *A map showing the location of the Danang beach, Pleiku, and La Drang, site of the first major conflict.*

numbers of ground troops to Vietnam. On March 8, 1965, marines landed at Danang beach in central Vietnam, quickly followed by thousands more marines and support forces. Although it was never formally declared, the United States was effectively at war with North Vietnam. President Johnson convinced American allies including Australia, South Korea and New Zealand to commit troops to the operation, but the United States supplied the overwhelming amount of manpower. By the end of the year, nearly 200,000 US troops were in the country. Hopes that

Rolling Thunder might halt the flow of Northern forces into the South were ill-founded as record numbers of troops continued to slip into South Vietnam. The influence of the Viet Cong was also growing. By the time the flamboyant but corrupt General Thieu became Head of State in South Vietnam in June 1965, it was estimated that they controlled up to 75 per cent of the South Vietnam countryside.

A SOLDIERS LIFE

Boot camp was often an horrific experience for soldiers, in which instructors used relentless physical and psychological abuse to mould their recruits into compliant soldiers (see

Sunday, Mar. 9, 1969

I'm sitting on the steps of our hooch looking out over the rice paddies and fields to the South. The Vietnamese are in the fields and paddies, working as they do every day... I don't know how to describe Vietnam or what it's like for me being here. It's totally alien is all I can say. There is no time for me to be myself. And I hope the extent of the changes that it will make on me will be minimal, and when I come home I'll be able to forget that I was ever here and return to my old self... My thoughts are mostly on Joanie and the time when I'll be home again. I think of our plans and what we will be doing once I get back to the States and can start living my life again. The first thing is for me to get back into school--that will be great. Next we will need some kind of a car and an apartment. Everything else will take care of itself.

Michael McAninch

 A letter home from US Marine Michael McAninch.

Below *Troops in Vietnam spent much of their day doing little, and had plenty of time to relax in a variety of ways.*

page 22). In Vietnam, life for many soldiers was a mixture of extreme boredom punctuated by moments of terror and exhilaration. Life on the ground in Vietnam could be quite comfortable. Accommodation varied from flimsy plywood buildings to proper wooden cabins, and there was plenty of time for relaxation and entertainment. Rock and roll provided a soundtrack to the soldier's experiences in Vietnam, and alcohol and drugs were also readily available. Racism, very much a part of life in 1960s America, usually evaporated in the muddy realities of the Vietnam jungle where everyone had to live together and fight for each other. When soldiers were called into combat, it was like nothing even seasoned soldiers had experienced before. Apart from the difficulty of negotiating a landscape of vines and swamps which was totally alien to American forces, the ground was often booby trapped. One soldier described how the effect was "sometimes like paralysis... you walk like a wooden man... with your eyes pinned to the dirt, spine arched, and you are shivering, shoulders hunched."

Above *Stores set up to serve GIs were run by locals. Some were friendly to the Americans, but others resented their presence.*

LA DRANG

The first proper battle between North Vietnamese and American forces took place around the la Drang valley. When NVA forces attacked a camp in the South, the US 1st Cavalry division and the ARVN drove them back to the valley. General Westmoreland ordered his troops to track down and kill the NVA soldiers. By the end of the confrontation 305 Americans and 3,561 NVA troops had been killed. Although la Drang seemed to be a victory for the Americans, it made the North

TIMELINE 1965

APRIL 6, 1965
President Johnson orders US troops to carry out offensive operations to support South Vietnamese forces.

APRIL 7, 1965
President Johnson offers talks with North Vietnam.

Above *United States' troops were given pocket guides to Vietnam to help them get to know the country.*

APRIL 15, 1965
First demonstration against the war attracts 16,000 people on a march to the White House.

JUNE 19, 1965
Ky, the eighth South Vietnamese premier since Diem, is sworn in.

JULY 21-28, 1965
President Johnson escalates conflict, raising the number of soldiers drafted to 35,000 a month.

"I have asked the commanding general, General Westmoreland, what more he needs to meet this mounting aggression. He has told me. And we will meet his needs. We cannot be defeated by force of arms. We will stand in Vietnam... I have today ordered to Vietnam the Air Mobile Division and certain other forces which will raise our fighting strength from 75,000 to 125,000 men almost immediately. Additional forces will be needed later, and they will be sent as requested.

"This will make it necessary to increase our active fighting forces by raising the monthly draft call from 17,000 over a period of time to 35,000 per month, and for us to step up our campaign for voluntary enlistments."

Address by President Johnson on television, July 28, 1965.

7 June 68

Dear Mom and Dad

I am sorry for not writing. This is my 14th or 15th day in the field. I am on an operation south of Da Nang. The name of the operation is Allen Brook. Is there anything about it on the news? Its been going on since the 12th of last month. So far we've captured a lot of new weapons and tons of rice. June 5th things got a little rough on my company. We took 28 wounded and six dead. So our company is hurting for some new men. On my birthday things didn't go to good. One of my best friends who I met in Hawaii was shot twice in the stomach and he died the following afternoon. His name was Art Sinksen... I am so sick of fighting I've seen and helped to many boys my age or younger that was wounded or dead. I thank the Lord each morning I get up. Well I should be going on R&R any time. That's about it over here. So say hi to everyone and take care of yourselves. Bye for Now

All My Love
Your Son Stephen
P.S. Write Soon

✉ **A letter home from US Marine Stephen E. Austin**

Vietnamese move away from direct confrontations in favour of guerrilla warfare. General Giap's new tactic was to lure United States forces into the highlands where fighting was more difficult and more costly. The war also demonstrated that the North Vietnamese were willing to sustain casualty rates in pursuit of their goal that the American public would never have been willing to tolerate.

SEARCH AND DESTROY

Towards the end of 1966, General Westmoreland ordered the first of three large search and destroy missions. Operation Attleboro destroyed a key base camp northwest of Saigon, killing 3,130 communists and wounding 900, with 200 missing. Then in January, 1967, Operation Cedar Falls was launched. Its aim was to seize control of an area north-west of Saigon known as the Iron Triangle. Troops were dropped in to evacuate the village of Ben Suc, and then an aerial bombardment took place, followed by a wave of ground troops. Underground tunnels

Right *Both men and women fought for the NLF against United States' and ARVN troops.*

"We slept in hammocks in small thatched bamboo huts, and we held our meetings in deep underground tunnels, which also served as shelter against air raids. Informers in Saigon passed us intelligence, so we were able to decamp whenever the Americans and their South Vietnamese puppets planned operations in the area. Anyway, we could hear them coming, because big modern armies cannot move quietly. Still, we had some close shaves. Once, soon after I arrived, American airplanes dropped thousands of tons of bombs around us, but we weren't even scratched."

General Tran Do, North Vietnam army, from interview in Hanoi in 1981.

"You ask me what I thought of the Americans. We thought the Americans were handsome soldiers but looked as if they were made with flour... it was difficult for them to suffer all the hardships of the Vietnamese battle-front. When we had no water to drink, they had water for showers! We could suffer the hardships much better than they could. That was probably the main reason we won."

NVA soldiers' opinion of US soldiers, 1982.

Above *WO1 Chip Parker with one of the ARA aircraft flown in the la Drang operation in November 1965.*

TIMELINE 1965–1967

OCT-NOV, 1965
Battle of La Drang Valley takes place, the first major land battle of the conflict.

FEBRUARY 4, 1966
Televised hearings on the Vietnam war take place in America, headed by Senator J William Fulbright.

MARCH-APRIL, 1966
A wave of protests against the South Vietnamese government takes place, led by Buddhists and students.

JAN 8-26, 1967
Operation Cedar Falls takes place northeast of Saigon.

FEB 22-APRIL 1,1967
Operation Junction City takes place.

SEPT 3, 1967
Nguyen Van Thieu becomes the new president of South Vietnam.

were targeted and jungle was destroyed to remove cover. Despite these successes, enemy forces returned to the area soon after the soldiers left. This pattern was repeated after the final mission, Operation Junction City, when the enemy, who were used to local conditions, simply hid until the Americans had left.

THE STRUGGLE MOVEMENT

In the South, public unrest at the regime headed by Ky and Thieu was growing. The Struggle Movement, led by Buddhist monks and students, was furious at Ky's refusal to negotiate with Hanoi, his reluctance to include civilians in his government and the army's ties to America. When government troops opened fire on protesters in Hue and Danang, calls for Ky to resign intensified. The fact that America supported Ky's actions did little to raise its popularity. When the ARVN attacked Buddhist pagodas in May 1966, opposition broke out across the South and was not ended until June. The way in which the Thieu government dealt with protesters turned many South Vietnamese against them, the Americans and the war itself.

Western Union Telegram
---MR. AND MRS. ALBERT H. AUSTIN
4057 MAIN STREET, DENAIR CA

I DEEPLY REGRET TO CONFIRM THAT YOUR SON CORPORAL STEPHEN E. AUSTIN, USMC, DIED ON 8 JUNE 1968 IN THE VICINITY OF QUANG NAM, REPUBLIC OF VIETNAM. HE SUSTAINED GUNSHOT WOUNDS TO THE HEAD AND BODY FROM HOSTILE RIFLE FIRE WHILE ON AN OPERATION. THE FOLLOWING INFORMATION IS PROVIDED TO ASSIST YOU IN MAKING FUNERAL ARRANGEMENTS. HIS REMAINS WILL BE PREPARED, ENCASED, AND SHIPPED AT NO EXPENSE TO YOU, ACCOMPANIED BY AN ESCORT, EITHER TO A FUNERAL HOME OR TO A NATIONAL CEMETERY SELECTED BY YOU.

Telegram to the parents of US Marine Stephen E. Austin.

Above *One of millions of badges issued to try to gather support in the United States for the action in Vietnam.*

CHAPTER 3

CRISIS TURNING POINT

Above A "Teach-In" debate on President Johnson's policy in Vietnam, which was broadcast to college campuses across the country in 1965.

As more and more American troops poured into Vietnam, and as the number of casualties mounted, public sentiment against the war began to change. This, coupled with the fact that no end to the conflict seemed to be in sight and there was little progress on the battlefield for the United States, made the unthinkable thinkable; that for the first time in its history, the United States might not win a war.

ANTI-WAR SENTIMENT

As President Johnson continued to pour troops into Vietnam, public unease back home became more and more vocal. Soldiers returning home from the battlefield were astonished to find themselves being jostled by protesters, some of whom even spat at them. At a time of great upheaval in American society, with the civil rights movement, women's rights and other political issues, protesting against American involvement in Vietnam became part of a wider questioning of the role of government in people's lives. When Johnson authorised the Rolling Thunder bombing raids in the wake of the Gulf of Tonkin incident, a series of teach-ins was held across the country in protest. Many college professors, angry at Johnson's escalation of the war, held special lectures and classes to inform their students about what was happening in Vietnam. In 1967, a number of anti-

"I didn't make it all the way through the second tour because I was wounded for the second and third time. When I arrived home in California, I was treated like someone with the plague. I was spit on, yelled at, threatened and looked upon as a mass murderer. Getting back to Medford was great because my family, friends, and neighbors were glad to see me in good health.

If possible, and with the same political mindset that existed in the 60s, I wouldn't do it again. If this country were ever to be invaded or if our national interests were truly threatened, then yes, I would."

Gerald Cooper, Marine, interviewed in 1986.

Below Protestors burning draft cards during an anti-Vietnam War demo in January, 1967.

war campaigns took place, including Negotiation Now!, a program of advertisements in national newspapers against the war; and Vietnam Summer, an anti-war effort that literally took the struggle to people's doorsteps. Then on October 21, a protest called the March on the Pentagon drew almost 100,000 people. Many protesters were involved in angry exchanges with police, and a watching Defense Secretary Robert McNamara admitted: "Christ, yes, I was scared." At the 1968 Democratic National Convention a riot broke out between protesters and police.

THE DRAFT

The draft was a method by which the United States government conscripted fit civilians into the armed forces when there were shortages. Until 1969, college students were exempted from the draft, but there were other ways to escape service. These ranged from fleeing the country, to failing the draft physical. Some were openly defiant. In protests across the country in October 1967, draft cards were burned, and resistors from New York sent defaced draft cards to the Attorney General in Washington.

On December 1, 1969, the possibility of being drafted quite literally became a lottery. The process of conscription changed from drafting the oldest man first to selecting civilians according to their date of birth. In front of television cameras, 366 plastic capsules (representing the 365 days of the year,

> Thursday Nov 23rd
>
> Dear Teri,
>
> I'm sorry for not writing for such a long time. Now I am living in Toronto, Canada. I am married to a guy named Tom Connay. Boy, I know this is going to be all things you don't want to hear. We are living in Canada because Tom is a draft resistor. I respect his position immensely. We are planning to become Canadian citizens and renounce our American citizenship...
>
> Yours, Cynthia

Cynthia Payne wife of a draft resistor, writing in 1968. ✉

> "I stood up to screaming patriots, and burned my draft card. I protested and marched, screamed and cried, told my generation to stop, don't go, this was wrong. I ended up a CO (conscientious objector) doing two years of bedpans, not smoking dope in Canada. I think that I, and those like me, are the true patriots, the true dissenters, who tried to stop 50,000 of our generation from coming home in bags.
>
> Honor the resistor, honor the protesters, the real patriots, those with the guts to stand up to a country gone mad with blood lust and a government hooked on body counts, and for what? Where is our memorial, where is our GI Bill for being right? 'Nam affected me too, and changed my life, without being there. Think about it. Who was right? None of you HAD to go, you could have fought to stay home."
>
> **Dr. Barry Spatz (excerpts),**
> **Website interview 1992.** 🎤

TIMELINE 1967

SEPT 29, 1967
President Johnson again offers talks with North Vietnam, promising to stop the bombing in return for talks. His proposition is called the "San Antonio Formula." Thieu is elected president of South Vietnam the same year.

OCT 16-21, 1967
Massive anti-draft demonstrations take place in the United States. Folk singer Joan Baez is arrested in California.

OCT 21-23, 1967
The March on the Pentagon attracts 100,000 demonstrators in Washington, DC.

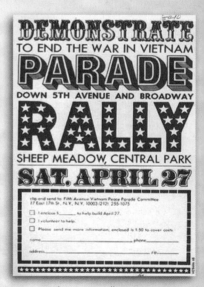

Above This 1970s rally poster attracted thousands of anti-war protesters in New York.

Above *The My Lai atrocity, where American soldiers massacred hundreds of unarmed villagers, turned many people against United States' actions in Vietnam.*

Above *United States' troops were issued with guidebooks which told them exactly how they should behave in warfare. Many of these ethics seemed to be lost in the battlefields of Vietnam.*

plus a leap day) were put into a container and picked out by hand, to determine the order of call for all men between the ages of 18-26 for the year of 1970. The draw continued until all the days had been given order numbers. The draft lottery continued until 1973, when conscription ended.

LOSING HEARTS AND MINDS

Because of the difficulty of measuring territorial gains in Vietnam, a system called bodycount was adopted by the American military to measure progress. This pursuit of numbers blurred the lines between civilians and soldiers on the battlefield, typified by the slogan adopted by some platoons – "If it's dead and Vietnamese, it's VC." This casual attitude to life was one of many factors that made Americans back home deeply concerned about the morality of the conflict. When an American platoon led by Lieutenant William Calley slaughtered 347 unarmed civilians at My Lai on March 16, 1968, revulsion was felt across the world. Soldiers' own accounts tell how women, children, the elderly, and even babies were killed by marauding soldiers. Calley was convicted of murder on March 29, 1971, but the massacre left an indelible

Hi everybody,

In one of your last letters you wanted to know more about the country. Well, scenery wise, the country is beautiful, except for the barbwire and bunkers spread out all over the countryside. The people themselves... make me sick. You learn not to trust them. I've been shot at by too many innocent looking people to have any mercy. They learn to fire a rifle even before they walk...

Paul O'Connoll, Marine, December 2, 1968

"I had heard of the dedication and focus of the enemy at all levels but to actually see it and finally to be shocked by an event on the battlefield was more then a "mind blower". It was THE moment in time that solidified my opposition to the position that the Old Men in the government had put us in. We had no prayer of doing anything positive in that country because the enemy was everyone - everyone either hated us or just wanted to be left alone to grow their rice. We should just fold up our money and go home."

 Marshall Darling, First Air Cavalry Khe Sanh Valley, 1968.

> "This is to notify you that an offensive and uprising will take place in the very near future and we will mount stronger attacks on towns and cities... The enemy will be thrown into utmost confusion. No matter how violently the enemy may react, he cannot avoid collapse. This is not only a golden opportunity to liberate hamlets and villages but also an opportunity to liberate district seas, province capitals and South Vietnam as a whole... Our victory is close at hand. The conditions are ripe. Our Party has carefully judged the situation. We must act and act fast. This is an opportunity to fulfil the aspirations of the entire people, of cadre, of each comrade and of our families..."

Directive to Communist forces for Tet Offensive, 1st November, 1967.

TIMELINE 1967-1968

DECEMBER, 1967
General Westmoreland declares "The enemy has been defeated at every turn."

JAN 20-APR 14, 1968
North Vietnamese troops attack US Khe Sanh base.

JAN 30, 1968
"Tet" offensive begins. North Vietnamese and NLF forces attack South Vietnamese cities.

MARCH 16, 1968
A US platoon kills hundreds of civilians at My Lai.

mark on the consciousness of the American public. Some soldiers claimed that to understand how such a thing could happen, you needed to experience the abuse suffered at boot camp, where, in the words of John Ketwig, men were "pushed, pulled, beaten, screamed at, humiliated, and emasculated for eight weeks", to understand that it could brutalize a man to the extent that he was rendered capable of committing such atrocities.

THE TET OFFENSIVE

At the beginning of 1968, troops from North Vietnam launched massive attacks on the South during Tet, Vietnam's most important holiday. The intention was to stop American bombing, force the collapse of the South Vietnamese government and maybe even force American withdrawal from Vietnam. The "Tet" strategy was to lure American troops into the countryside as a diversion, and then launch major attacks on the cities, in the hope of causing their populations to rebel and join the communist cause. NVA forces attacked the Marine base at Khe Sanh in north-west South Vietnam on 21st January. Johnson responded just as Ho Chi Minh had hoped he would, sending thousands of troops to defend the base, backed up by B-52 bombers. While this was happening, Northern forces attacked cities across the South. American and ARVN forces fought back and eventually managed to subdue the communists. Although the Americans appeared to come out on top, the number of United States forces who perished in the offensive made the American public realise just

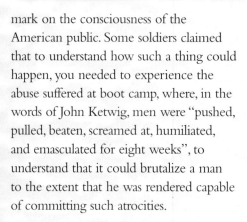

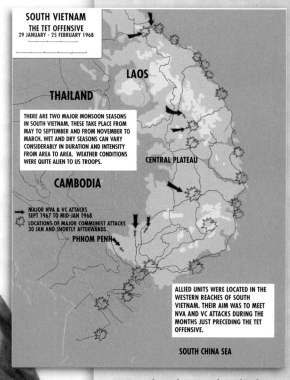

SOUTH VIETNAM
THE TET OFFENSIVE
29 JANUARY - 25 FEBRUARY 1968

LAOS

THAILAND

THERE ARE TWO MAJOR MONSOON SEASONS IN SOUTH VIETNAM. THESE TAKE PLACE FROM MAY TO SEPTEMBER AND FROM NOVEMBER TO MARCH. WET AND DRY SEASONS CAN VARY CONSIDERABLY IN DURATION AND INTENSITY FROM AREA TO AREA. WEATHER CONDITIONS WERE QUITE ALIEN TO US TROOPS.

CENTRAL PLATEAU

CAMBODIA

→ MAJOR NVA & VC ATTACKS SEPT 1967 TO MID-JAN 1968
✿ LOCATIONS OF MAJOR COMMUNIST ATTACKS 30 JAN AND SHORTLY AFTERWARDS

PHNOM PENH

ALLIED UNITS WERE LOCATED IN THE WESTERN REACHES OF SOUTH VIETNAM. THEIR AIM WAS TO MEET NVA AND VC ATTACKS DURING THE MONTHS JUST PRECEDING THE TET OFFENSIVE.

SOUTH CHINA SEA

Above The red arrows show the decoy attack that preceded the Tet Offensive and the jagged circles the main battles of the actual Offensive.

Left NVA troops resting during the "Tet" offensive.

Above *United States marines exchange fire during the Tet Offensive in 1968.*

Below *A map showing the US invasion route into Cambodia.*

how bloody the war was. The North Vietnamese leader General Giap summed up the situation by saying that until Tet they had thought they could win the war, but "now they knew that they could not."

SCALING DOWN

The bloodshed at Tet brought about a shift in American policy. President Johnson made a speech saying that bombing in North Vietnam would be restricted, and that America would negotiate with Hanoi. Talks between representatives of both sides were initiated and continued for the next five years. Despite this, in early 1968, American operations in South Vietnam accelerated as Johnson became increasingly fearful that the South Vietnamese government would collapse. Efforts to encourage South Vietnamese forces to take on a greater share of the fighting met with limited success; they were increasingly de-motivated and reluctant to fight in a war that many were not sure why they were fighting.

NIXON AND NEGOTIATION

Although he had previously been a firm supporter of the Vietnam war and a politician renowned for his anti-communist views, Richard Nixon's election as President in 1968 ushered in the beginning of the end of the conflict. The bloodshed at Tet and the reaction to it back home convinced Nixon to run for election on a platform of "peace with honor". The plan was to engineer an honorable American exit that would leave the South Vietnamese to stand firm against the communists – a shifting of responsibility Nixon called Vietnamization. Between 1969-1971, while announcing troop withdrawals to the American public Nixon used his "madman" theory – an effort to make Ho Chi Minh think that he might do anything to win the war – to try to force Hanoi to negotiate. He hoped that this might allow him to achieve the best peace terms possible. The first stage of Nixon's strategy was the bombing of the Ho Chi Minh Trail, and secret attacks on Vietnamese bases in Cambodia. Then, when a pro-

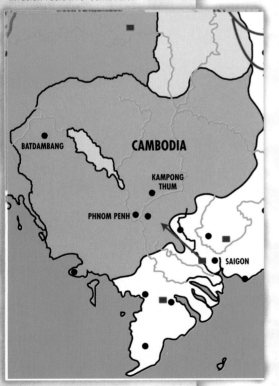

1st April, 1969,

Dear Professor Coffman,

How odd of me it is not to have written to you before this... As the months have gone by (7 now) I've been trying to compare what I read in the American and foreign press to what I've actually observed. My position is... this is a war begun strictly by political elements in the American Congress. The authorization they receive to act under the Gulf of Tonkin resolution was artificially expanded to pronounce a mandate of military measures. In short, there was much pressure on Congress into letting them flex a little muscle. The Vietnamese are an illiterate people, who have little sense of Nationhood. They do not care to die for a cause which appears imposed by Westerners.... Therefore the desertion rate is still horrendously high. Most of my good friends here feel that their sacrifice is not appreciated. As for the Saigon government, I personally feel that it will not last there after we have gone... Vietnam has not been worth the price. War has never been productive, and our investment here will reap very little return.

Heroically yours, Benjamin.

Letter to University of Wisconsin-Madison history professor Edward Coffman from a former student.

American faction led by Lon Nol seized power in Cambodia, Nixon decided to send up to 30,000 US and ARVN troops across the border to aid Nol's fight against North Vietnamese insurgents, while also mounting an attack on a supposed Vietnamese Communist office in Cambodia (the COSVN). The invasion of Cambodia led to protests across several university campuses in the United States, two of which ended in tragedy. On May 4, 1970, the National Guard shot dead four anti-war protesters at Kent State University in Ohio. Then on May 14, two students at Jackson State University, Mississippi, were killed by police. Nixon's response to the outrage that followed was to announce that all American troops would be pulled out of Cambodia by June. This did not stop Nixon extending the war again in February 1971. Against the advice of General Westmoreland, Nixon sent ARVN troops supported by American air power into Laos to attack North Vietnamese insurgents. The invasion was a disaster – the ARVN were decimated, raising serious doubts as to whether the South Vietnamese could ever win a war against the North without the Americans.

PENTAGON PAPERS

In 1971, Nixon suffered a further blow when government documents known as the Pentagon Papers were leaked to The New York Times and The Washington Post. Commissioned by Robert McNamara in early 1967, they detail decision-making during the Vietnam War. The documents showed that America's leaders had broken

"How long would it take to succeed in Vietnam? They didn't know. How many more troops would it take? They couldn't say. Were two hundred thousand the answer? They weren't sure. Might they need more? Yes, they might need more. Could the enemy build up in in exchange? Probably. So what was the plan to win the war? Well the only plan was that attrition would wear out the Communists, and they would have had enough. Was there any indication that we've reached that point? No, there wasn't."

Defense Secretary Clifford speaking to Stanley Karnow about war plans just before the Tet Offensive.

international agreements, manipulated the South Vietnamese government and also lied to Congress and the American Public about how badly the war was going. Nixon's chance re-election in the 1972 presidential elections seemed slim.

TIMELINE 1969-1970

MARCH 18, 1969
President Nixon begins policy of "Vietnamization".

SEPT 2, 1969
Ho Chi Minh dies.

MARCH 27, 1970
ARVN forces attack Communist bases in Cambodia.

MAY 4, 1970
Four protestors are killed at Kent State University of the Ohio National Guard troops.

Left *Student Mary Ann Vecchio kneels over the body of fellow student Jeffrey Miller, shot by the National Guard during an anti-war protest at Kent State University, Ohio.*

Above *A 1972 Youth International Party (Yippie) pin-back button with an orange and blue yin-yang symbol from an anti-Vietnam War rally.*

CHAPTER 4

AFTERMATH END OF THE CONFLICT

> "The United States and all other countries respect the independence, sovereignty, unity and territorial integrity of Vietnam as recognized by the 1954 Geneva Agreements on Vietnam." (Article 1)
>
> "A cease-fire shall be observed throughout South Vietnam as of 2400 hours, GMT, on January 27th, 1973." (Article 2)
>
> "The United States will not continue its military involvement or intervene in the internal affairs of South Vietnam." (Article 4).
>
> "The South Vietnamese people shall decide themselves the political future of South Vietnam through genuinely free and democratic general elections under international supervision." (Article 9)
>
> *Extracts from the Paris Peace Accords, 27th January 1973*

By the middle of 1972 the United States government was coming to the realization that the war in Vietnam could not be won. Equally, the North Vietnamese were keen to break the stalemate that had existed in the country since the Tet Offensive. With both sides seemingly ready to compromise, the stage was set for negotiation, and by the beginning of 1973, an agreement was in place that would see all United States troops leave Vietnam by the end of the year.

THE ROAD TO PARIS

Four years after the "Tet' Offensive, General Giap ordered another massive invasion of South Vietnam in an attempt to end the war. The Easter Offensive saw more than 100,000 troops pour southwards hoping to overwhelm an enemy still shaken by events in Laos. Despite initial successes, however, North Vietnam's hopes for a quick victory were dashed by a massive American retaliatory bombing campaign called Operation Linebacker. With a stalemate still in evidence, both sides were beginning to realise that a diplomatic solution might be the only way to resolve the situation. Following secret talks between top officials from both sides,

Above *American prisoners of war reporting to US representatives at Gia Lam Airport in Hanoi.*
Bottom left *Even after the cease-fire, fighting continued in South Vietnam.*

FEB 8, 1971
South Vietnamese troops begin unsuccessful campaign to cut off Ho Chi Minh Trail in Laos.

JUNE 13, 1971
The Pentagon Papers are published by the New York Times.

DEC 26, 1971
President Nixon orders troops to start bombing North Vietnam again.

MAR 30-APR 8, 1972
The Easter Offensive begins.

OCT 8-11, 1972
Kissinger and Le Duc Tho agree settlement to war, later rejected by South Vietnam.

DEC 18-31, 1972
The US Christmas bombing begins.

Le Duc Tho's "framework for peace" – a cease-fire followed by US withdrawal – was approved by Nixon's National Security Advisor, Henry Kissinger, and plans were made to make things official after Nixon's re-election. But when South Vietnam objected to the terms of the plan, Kissinger put forward amendments which resulted in talks being temporarily abandoned. Nixon sent aircraft and armoured vehicles to the South to put pressure on Thieu to renegotiate, followed up by bombing during December 18 on Hanoi and Haiphon. The two sides eventually resumed negotiations and on January 27, 1973 the Paris Agreement was signed. While it signalled an end to an American presence in Vietnam the agreement failed to provide any clarity as to the precarious future of South Vietnam.

AMERICAN WITHDRAWAL

American troop numbers in South Vietnam began to dwindle even before the Paris Agreement was signed, but the process accelerated during 1973. South Vietnam released 27,000 prisoners of war, while North Vietnam released 591 US prisoners of war and more than 5,000 South Vietnamese

Larry Chesley, POW for almost eight years.

February 12 was a beautiful day in North Vietnam, - at least to 112 American POWs. We had received our going away clothes the night before and cleaned up our rooms as well as we could. We assembled in the courtyard and made our way under guard to the gate of the Hanoi Hilton. This was the first time we had moved anywhere from there without being blindfolded and handcuffed.

Excerpt from Seven Years in Hanoi by Larry Chesley.

Above *Despite Nixon's victory in the 1972 Presidential elections, he resigned in disgrace after the Watergate scandal broke.*

"Today, with boundless joy, throughout the country our 45 million people are jubilantly celebrating the great victory we have won in the general offensive and uprising this Spring of 1975, in completely defeating the war of aggression and the neo-colonialist rule of US imperialism, liberating the whole of the southern half of our country so dear to our hearts and gloriously ending the longest, most difficult and greatest patriotic war ever waged in the history of our people's struggle against foreign aggression... We hail the new era in our nation's 4,000 year history - era of brilliant prospects for the development of a peaceful, independent, reunified, democratic, prosperous and strong Viet Nam, an era in which the laboring people have become the complete masters of their destiny and will pool their physical and mental efforts to build a plentiful and happy life for themselves and for thousands of generations to come."

Le Duan's victory speech, 15th May 1975, Hanoi

Below *Vietnamese soldiers commemorate the 25th anniversary of the fall of the pro-American regime in Saigon.*

captives were set free. A bill in Congress committed Nixon to withdrawing all troops by August 15, 1973. The only Americans left behind after this would be civilians. Despite this, relations between North and South Vietnam remained as bad as ever. ARVN forces continued to fight throughout 1973 as Thieu refused to negotiate with communists, adopting a policy he called the "Four No's". Senior figures in the South remained fearful about Nixon's commitment to protect the right of self-determination in South Vietnam. At the same time, appalling economic conditions in South Vietnam and demonstrations from Buddhists and other groups against their policies further weakened the position of the Saigon government. Believing that the American authorities might not protect Saigon, Thieu ordered NVA troops to head southwards. After gaining Phuoc Long in the highlands and then Pleiku and Kontum, North Vietnamese troops were rampant. The South Vietnamese army simply fell apart and hundreds of thousands of refugees tried to flee. The decision not to intervene was made by the

Above *A CIA employee helps evacuees onto an Air America helicopter from the top of 22 Gia Long Street, a half mile from the U.S. Embassy.*

JAN 23, 1973
President Nixon proclaims the signing of the Paris Agreement.

FEB, 1973
American prisoners of war start to be released.

MAR, 1973
The last American combat soldiers leave North Vietnam.

FEB, 1975
North Vietnamese offensive against Saigon begins.

AUG 9, 1975
Nixon resigns after Watergate. President Ford takes charge.

new president of the United States Gerald Ford, and the last Americans were whisked away from Saigon in helicopters as the communists approached, a humiliating end to a war that had cost the lives of almost 60,000 Americans and millions of Vietnamese from both sides of the divide. The jubilant Hanoi government renamed Saigon Ho Chi Minh city in memory of their most famous leader.

Saigon, South Vietnam, April 30 - Communist troops of North Vietnam and the Provisional Revolutionary Government of South Vietnam poured into Saigon today as a century of Western influences came to an end.

In Paris, representatives of the Provisional Revolutionary Government announced that Saigon had been renamed Ho Chi Minh City in honor of the late President of North Vietnam. Other representatives said in a broadcast monitored in Thailand that former Government forces in eight provinces south of the capital had not yet surrendered, but no fighting was mentioned.

The transfer of power was symbolized by the raising of the flag of the National Liberation Front over the presidential palace at 12:15pm today, about two hours after General Minh's surrender broadcast.

The New York Times, April 30, 1975

Above *In February 1975, NVA troops began to flood southwards.*

CHAPTER 5

POPULAR CULTURE THE WAR IN THE MEDIA

Below *Robert De Niro starred as the mentally unstable Vietnam war veteran Travis Bickle in the 1976 film Taxi Driver.*

From the early 1960s, Vietnam loomed large in the public consciousness, and was brought to public attention in a variety of mediums. Television broadcasts, and films such as The Deer Hunter, Apocalypse Now, Taxi Driver *and the* Rambo *movies offered very different interpretations of events in Asia, while musicians ranging from Bob Dylan to Jimi Hendrix railed against the war through their songs.*

THE WAR ON FILM

Although films had been made about the troubles in Vietnam since the beginning of the war, large scale releases did not follow until much later. The war was increasingly unpopular with the American public, and as a result the subject was shunned by many Hollywood film makers. Then in the 1970s, a series of films looking at the conflict were released. *Taxi Driver* (1976) portrayed the returning soldier as damaged and deranged by the war. In Francis Ford Coppola's *Apocalypse Now* (1979) a man searches for an American colonel who has disappeared in the jungles of Vietnam. When he finds him, he discovers a man who lives only to kill the North Vietnamese enemy, a figure on the brink of savagery. In the 1980s the trilogy of Rambo movies starring Sylvester Stallone showed another trend in Vietnam films – the idea that the American marine had been prevented from winning the war by the United States administration. *Platoon*, released in 1986, offered the public a glimpse at the day to day life for soldiers in Vietnam, and in 1987, Stanley Kubrick's *Full Metal Jacket* looked at how the brutalising experience of American boot camp and the culture there could make men capable of committing such atrocities as My Lai. More recently, Oliver Stone's *Born on the Fourth of July* (1989) reflected the changing public view of Vietnam veterans through the eyes of disabled veteran Ron Kovic. In Stone's film, Kovic suffers humiliation at boot camp and terrible injury on the battlefield, and returns to rejection at home, only finding redemption and acceptance more than a decade later when the public began

> Day by day I struggle to maintain not only my strength but also my sanity. It's all a blur. I have no energy to write. I don't know what is right or wrong anymore. The morale of the men is low, a civil war in the platoon.
>
> Somebody once wrote: "Hell is the impossibility of reason." That's what this place feels like. Hell.
>
> (Chris Taylor)
>
> *Excerpt from the film* **Platoon** *(1986) by* **Oliver Stone.**

OFFICIAL SPEECH · GOVERNMENT DOCUMENT · NEWSPAPER ARTICLE · INTERVIEW

Above *The slogan for Oliver Stone's 1986 film Platoon encapsulated the moral problems many soldiers faced in Vietnam. "The first casualty of war is innocence".*

APRIL 30, 1975

The US trade embargo is extended to cover all Vietnam.

JULY, 1976

Vietnam was formally reunified in July, 1976.

More than 600,000 people are moved from Ho Chi Minh City to rural areas in a resettlement plan.

DEC, 1978

Vietnam invades Cambodia and topples Pol Pot's Khmer Rouge government, ending its reign of terror.

1979

Western European countries and non-communist Asian nations support US-led embargo against Vietnam, in protest against invasion of Cambodia.

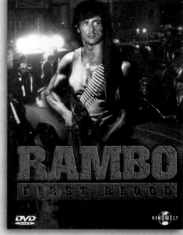

Above *A video cover of the 1982 film Rambo. It stars Sylvester Stallone as the persecuted Vietnam Vet John Rambo.*

In the last month of school, the marine recruiters came and spoke to my senior class... It was like all the movies and all the books and all the dreams of becoming a hero come true. "Good afternoon, men", the tall marine said. "We have come today because they told us that some of you want to become marines." He told us that the marines took nothing but the best... The tall marine spoke in a very beautiful way about the exciting history of the marines and how they had never lost and American had never been defeated... As I shook their hands and stared up into their eyes, I couldn't help but feel I was shaking hands with John Wayne and Audie Murphy. (Ron Kovic)

Excerpt from* Born on the Fourth of July *(1989) by Ron Kovic.

Below *Bob Dylan was a key figure in the anti-war movement.*

to realise the bravery of the veteran who fought for the government. The Vietnamese war was also captured on film by North Vietnamese cameramen. Numerous documentaries were shown in Vietnam and other communist countries but were hidden from the West. Today, there are plans to make many of these recordings available to people outside Vietnam for the very first time.

THE WAR ON VINYL

From the moment the conflict in Vietnam began, popular music in the United States began to reflect the tensions it provoked. Famous protest songs of the era included "Last Train to Clarksville" by The Monkees, about a man on his way to an army base, knowing he may die in Vietnam ("I don't know if I'm ever coming home") and Creedence Clearwater Revival's "Senator's Son", the tale of a working-class soldier unable to dodge the draft because he "ain't no Senator's son". Protest through music continued at the Woodstock festival held during 1969. Many of the acts who performed there made anti-war speeches, including Joan Baez and Country Joe. Then after the Kent State University shootings in 1970, "Ohio" by Crosby, Stills, Nash and Young angrily attacked the actions of the National Guard. Not all musicians were against the war, however. Artists including Johnny Cash stood up for the soldiers fighting in Vietnam, saluting their bravery in defending their country and criticising the actions of the protestors who jeered them on their return home.

ARTISTS AND THE WAR

Art also played an important role in shaping opinions during the war. During the Vietnam War the US Army sent teams of soldier artists into the field to record a visual record of their experiences. The art they

I got a friend named Whiskey Sam
He was my boonierat buddy for a year in Nam
He said is my country just a little off track
Took 'em twenty-five years to welcome me back
It was a real slow walk in a real sad rain
And nobody tried to be John Wayne
I came home, but Tex did not
And I can't talk about the hit he got
I got a little limp now when
I walk Got a little tremolo when
I talk But my letter read from Whiskey Sam
You're a walkin' talkin' miracle from Vietnam

🎵 *Drive On, by Johnny Cash (1963).*

"How many roads must a man walk down
Before you call him a man?
Yes, 'n' how many seas must a white dove sail
Before she sleeps in the sand?
Yes, 'n' how many times must the cannon balls fly
Before they're forever banned?
The answer, my friend, is blowin' in the wind,
The answer is blowin' in the wind."

🎵 *Blowin' in the Wind, by Bob Dylan(1963).*

Above *Oil painting by R.G. Smith showing three Vietnamese awaiting questioning on the deck of a patrol boat.*

FEB, 1979
Suspicious of Vietnamese relations with the Soviet Union after the Treaty of Friendship and Cooperation in 1978, China decides to invade Vietnam.

1982
About 120,000 former members of the former Saigon regime, plus critics of the new government and other minorities, are now being held in "re-education camps".

created is now on display in the US Army's Center of Military History Army Art Collection. Navy combat artists also recorded the scenes they witnessed to make a record of their experiences. The war also provided rich pickings for satirical artists around the world. Artists such as Herbert Block of *The Washington Post* published weekly cartoons that drew public attention to what was happening in Vietnam. These would frequently be highly critical of American policies towards Vietnam and the actions of presidents such as Richard Nixon.

Above *Satirical illustration by Herbert Block of The Washington Post, published August 9, 1972, mocking Nixon's 1968 promise to end the war in Vietnam.*

MARCH, 1982
Vietnamese Communist Party (VCP) Fifth National Party Congress held. Leaders admit mistakes have been made in rebuilding the country.

HEADQUARTERS
20TH GENERAL SUPPORT GROUP
US ARMY ASCOM DISTRICT
APO SAN FRANCISCO 96220

Sp instr: Upon completion of TDY in Vietnam EM is placed on 75 days dy w/SSO, Hq USARHAW, APO SF 96557... Indiv must havein poss basic req summer unif, work unif & cbt boots. Plague immun req but tvl WNB delayed except for 1st vaccine dose. Bording pass DA Form 1472 will be reequ for MAC flight overseas. Indiv WB equip w/m17 protective mask & corr lenses if nec prior to dprt this comd. ID tags WB worn while tvl by mil aircraft. Indiv w/have cy of immun rec & valid ID card in poss at all times. Bag alw 66 lbs; personal eff, and an ex bag alw of 30 lbs for art supplies and technical equip. Combat pay of $65.00 per month will be auth while on duty in Vietnam. Per diem will be in accord with JTR.

Telegram authorizing supply of art materials to a soldier artist serving in Vietnam.

Above This certificate marks the bravery of Canadian Lawrence M Dickens, who helped to rescue Vietnamese boat people.

Thirty years after the end of the Vietnam war, the issue continues to provoke debate in the United States and around the world. After American troops left Vietnam, the battered and bombed country had to begin the process of rebuilding. Back home, veterans had to take their place in society, and the United States had to take another look at its position in the world. Today, with the collapse of the Cold War, relations between the two countries have been restored, but the issue of Vietnam has not disappeared.

Right An American plane drops the chemical Agent Orange over North Vietnamese jungle. It was used to strip foliage under which enemy troops might otherwise hide in.

"Affected areas covered 120 kilometers east-west and 150 kilometers north-south. Five minutes was all that was needed to wither tapioca, sweet potato… and banana plants. Livestock suffered heavy injuries… Most of the river fish were found lying dead on the surface of mountain streams and brooks. The three days of chemical attack poisoned scores of people, took the lives of about 10 and inflicted a "natus" disease (with symptoms like a severe rash) upon 18,000 inhabitants."

Vietnamese peasant described a three-day chemical attack near DaNang in February 1966

THE LEGACY IN VIETNAM

For the next 20 years the country would be one of the poorest in the world, due to the damage inflicted by the war and also the disastrous economic policies implemented by the communist regime. In neighbouring Cambodia, the US-backed Lon Nol government collapsed and the Khmer Rouge rose to power, initiating a genocide that claimed the lives of 1.7 million people, or about 26 per cent of the population. When hundreds of thousands of Cambodian refugees poured over the border to Vietnam, the

Hanoi government decided to invade Cambodia, provoking an attack from Cambodia's ally China. More than 50,000 Vietnamese people had died by the time troops finally left Cambodia in 1991.

A POISONED LANDSCAPE?

The Vietnam war left a deadly legacy that stayed long after American troops went home. Agent Orange, a chemical cocktail containing the poison dioxin, was sprayed over the jungle by American forces to remove cover where Viet Cong troops might hide. Today, the rates of cancer in Vietnam are much higher than in surrounding countries and doctors attribute this to the effects of Agent Orange. The chemical also had a highly damaging effect on farming, as areas stripped by the chemical were overrun by weeds. Another dangerous legacy of the war are the land mines that lurk everywhere in the Vietnamese landscape. In some places, the ground is studded with unexploded shells that explode when land is farmed or sometimes if it is just walked over.

PERSECUTED PEOPLE

Between 1975 and 1990, more than a million frightened Vietnamese fled the country, many seeking refuge in the United States. Some were so desperate to escape they left in tiny fishing boats to sail to freedom, gaining the name

" I saw hundreds of people trying to escape the thick black smoke rising up into the grey sky. All our homes, the entire village was in flames. People had grabbed what belongings they could carry before they left. Some had bicycles to carry their possessions, others had baskets or pushed carts. Little children were carried by older brothers and sisters or pulled along by harassed mothers, arms full of bundles.

When we got into the boat, I liked watching fish swimming in the water, and all the boats around us. It was like an adventure for me. I did not understand what was really happening. My mum was holding my little sister and she was crying, but I didn't understand, I was too excited."

Anh and Kim's account of escaping Vietnam.

LEFT *After the American exit, thousands of boat people fled the country, fearful of the new Communist regime.*

TIMELINE 1982-1987

NOV 11, 1982
The Vietnam Veterans' Memorial, "The Wall", is dedicated in Washington, DC.

1985
The Hanoi government admits it is still holding 10,000 inmates in re-education camps. Some people believe the real number is 40,000. Ho Chi Minh City mayor Mai Chi Tho tells Western reporters that "socialist transition" will not be complete until the year 2000.

AUG 1-3, 1987
Special Envoy of President Reagan, General John Vesey visits Vietnam to discuss humanitarian issues of mutual interest.

Above *After waves of boat people left Vietnam for the United States, many settled and had children. These Amerasian children are a reminder of the history between Vietnam and the United States.*

Above *The Vietnam Memorial Wall was dedicated in November of 1982. The tradition of leaving gifts at the base of the wall began before the Wall was even completed.*

"boat people". Many of those South Vietnamese who stayed behind found themselves persecuted by the new regime because of their collusion with United States troops. Hundreds of thousands of South Vietnamese were imprisoned and tortured by the communist authorities, or sent to concentration camps. Employment prospects for South Vietnamese and their children who had helped the Americans were also severely hampered, because the new regime forced them to declare this fact when applying for jobs. For the many Vietnamese women who gave birth to children conceived by relationships with American soldiers during the war, life in the new Vietnam was even harder. Mixed-race children were given the name "con lai" (half-breed) or "bui doi" (the dust of life), while their mothers were frowned upon by Vietnamese society. Because it was very difficult to leave Vietnam after 1975, there was no option of joining their fathers in America. But in 1987, with relations between the United States and Vietnam improving, the US congress passed the Amerasian Homecoming Act. By 1994, 25,000 Amerasians had arrived in the United States.

VETS AND THE WALL

When American forces returned from the war, many found it very hard to settle back into civilian life. Some suffered mental illness as a result of what they had experienced in the jungles of South East Asia, and had to cope in a society which initially showed little sympathy to their plight. Those in need of medical help often found themselves treated harshly by doctors. Divorce, alcoholism and even homelessness remain rife amongst veterans. Today it is estimated that about a quarter of all homeless people on the streets of America are Vietnam veterans. The process of acceptance back into American society began in 1982 with the construction of the Vietnam war memorial in Washington.

The wall begins with the inscription: "IN HONOR OF THE MEN AND WOMEN OF THE ARMED FORCES OF THE UNITED STATES WHO SERVED IN THE VIETNAM WAR. THE NAMES OF THOSE WHO GAVE THEIR LIVES AND OF THOSE WHO REMAIN MISSING ARE INSCRIBED IN THE ORDER THEY WERE TAKEN FROM US" on panel 1E, goes out to the end of the East wall, appears to recede into the earth (70E, May 25, 1968), resumes at the end of the West wall as it emerges from the earth (70W, continuing May 25, 1968) and ends with the date 1975 and inscription: "OUR NATION HONORS THE COURAGE, SACRIFICE AND DEVOTION TO DUTY AND COUNTRY OF ITS VIETNAM VETERANS. THIS MEMORIAL WAS BUILT WITH PRIVATE CONTRIBUTIONS FROM THE AMERICAN PEOPLE. NOVEMBER 11, 1982)

**The Vietnam Veterans'
Memorial Wall, Washington, DC**

August 23, 2000 ~ Response from Senator John Warner

Thank you for your letter concerning Prisoners of War and Missing in Action service members. Your accounting of Wade Lynn Ellen is tragic and, as you concluded, is an unfinished event that deserves to be resolved.

There have been several initiatives before the 106th Congress to address the issue of Prisoners of War and Missing in Action service members. These measures include:

House Concurrent Resolution 311: Expresses the sense of Congress that the United States should continue to actively pursue efforts to achieve a full accounting of all members of the Armed Forces who remain unaccounted for from previous conflicts, particularly the Korean War and the Vietnam War, and to continue and maintain programs and procedures for achieving a full accounting of all military personnel who become prisoners of war or missing in action in future conflicts.

Once again I thank you for contacting me on this very important matter, and I am moved by the concern and compassion you displayed for a fellow American.

Kind Regards,

Senator Warner

SEP 29, 1990
Foreign Minister Nguyen Co Thach meets Secretary of State James Baker in New York.

NOV 11, 1991
The US Government officially allows American tourists, veterans, journalists, businessmen to visit Vietnam.

NOV 1994
President Clinton visits Hanoi and receives a warm welcome. The American embargo on Vietnam is lifted the same year.

Above *Many Vietnam veterans, no longer made to feel ashamed of their involvement in the war, wear badges to signify their service in Vietnam.*

JAN 27, 1995
The United States and Vietnam establish liaison offices in each other's capitals.

JULY 11, 1995
President Clinton announces normalization of relations with Vietnam.

Designed by Maya Ying Lin, it bears the names of 58,325 American soldiers killed in Vietnam.

THE MIA ISSUE

After the war ended, many American soldiers were still unaccounted for. They were categorized "missing in action" (MIA). A survey shortly after the war revealed that more than 60 per cent of Americans thought that MIAs were still being held in North Vietnamese prisons. Teams of Americans were sent to Vietnam to search for bodies, digging up graves in cemeteries. Authorities in Hanoi allowed this in the hope of fostering better relations between the two countries, but ordinary Vietnamese were offended by American actions, particularly when bodies of their relatives were disturbed in the process. Today, a few Americans still believe that soldiers are being held prisoner in North Vietnam.

Left *US servicemen and women carry a coffin containing the remains of a soldier recovered in Vietnam's central provinces. Around 1,800 American personnel are listed as missing in action.*

Below *American veteran of the Vietnam war Bill Dyke hugs his former enemy, retired North Vietnamese army soldier Mai Thuan during a ground-breaking meeting between veterans on both sides of the former conflict, in Hanoi, April 26, 2000.*

RELATIONS WITH VIETNAM

The United States and the Vietnamese governments were not willing to consider repairing relations for many years after the war ended. When Vietnam invaded Cambodia, the United States, together with Western European countries, placed an embargo against Vietnam, and as recently as 1991 the United States prevented the International Monetary Fund (IMF) granting economic aid to Vietnam. But in the 1980s, contact began to grow, helped by Vietnamese cooperation over the MIA issue and Vietnam's withdrawal from Cambodia. In 1991 the United States and Vietnam agreed to establish an office in Hanoi to help to determine the fate of MIAs , and Washington gave Hanoi a road-map towards the restoration of normal relations. Later that year, the United States lifted a ban on its citizens travelling to Vietnam. Then in 1994, President Clinton lifted the US trade embargo with Vietnam, and the following year diplomatic relations were restored. Misunderstandings still occur – an American plan to open a burger chain called Uncle Ho's Hamburgers was not well received – but tourism is now one of the biggest industries in Vietnam.

US FOREIGN POLICY

It can be argued that the Vietnam war had a marked effect on American foreign policy and made the United States more hesitant to commit forces abroad. Public opinion during the 1980s remained resolutely against America becoming involved in "another Vietnam" and polls showed that most people were deeply concerned about possible American involvement in Central America.

Had it not been for Vietnam, President Reagan would have had US troops in Nicaragua and probably several other places. Because of Vietnam the American people would have none of it so it didn't happen. Those of us who think the Vietnam war was a terrible mistake should carefully consider how we feel about the Americans who fought there. We should take that thought one step further and realize that many individual soldiers were fighting for their country. They did heroic things for their country. They died for their country. A sacrifice for a cause you believe is right is no less a sacrifice because ten years later it turns out not to be right. Those soldiers' intent was to fight for their country and that intent was noble.

14:00:30 US/Eastern 1996)
Terry Crenshaw, a Vietnam protestor posted to Vietnam website, 1996.

Above *A crowd hold up signs protesting against US military intervention in the first Gulf War.*

It was not until the First Gulf War in 1991 that America made another significant commitment of troops abroad. Following victory, President George Bush's comment: "By God, we've kicked the Vietnam Syndrome once and for all!" showed a new outlook. The United States then sent forces abroad to Kosovo in the 1990s and to Afghanistan and Iraq in 2003–2004. Politically, a Vietnam service record became a badge of honour, rather than something to be ashamed of. This was shown most recently in the 2004 Presidential Elections, when President George W. Bush faced allegations of draft dodging, while Democrat candidate John Kerry publicised his war record and presented himself as a war hero. This claim, was refuted by some servicemen who questioned some of the Purple Hearts collected by Kerry while serving in Vietnam, and George W Bush went on to secure another term in the White House.

"Beloved, I continue to feel the pain and anguish and loss as deeply as the day I was told you were gone. The new friends I have made, the McAninch family I have recovered, the restored letters and photographs to replace my lost mementos, the web sites I have created for you and them--all have provided solace and some respite for my aching heart. But when you went down into that Valley, when you went back to defend your Marine brothers, my hand was in yours: I went with you; I feel the mortar fragments searing my own chest and back every day, and I groan and rage against the pain and unfairness of your tragedy. Part of me, the best part of me, never returned from Vietnam either. Nothing, nothing can ever replace you in my life."

Letter from Joan McAninch to Michael McAninch, a marine killed in action in 1969. ✉

TIMELINE 1995-

AUG 5, 1995
US Embassy in Hanoi opened by Secretary of State Warren Christopher.

APRIL 10, 1997
Former POW Douglas "Pete" Peterson becomes the first ambassador to Vietnam since the end of the war.

OCT 3, 2001
The United States Senate approves an agreement normalizing trade between the United States and Vietnam.

Above *Today visitors from the United States go to Vietnam as tourists, where they are welcomed by the Vietnamese people.*

NOV 10, 2003
US Secretary of Defense Donald Rumsfeld meets Vietnam's Defense Minister Pham Van Tra.

NOV 19, 2003
Navy missile frigate USS Vandegrift docks at Ho Chi Minh City, a symbolic act intended to boost relations between Vietnam and the United States.

he Vietnam War was run by major personalities on both sides. On the American side, presidents from Eisenhower to Nixon made major decisions about the war that changed the course of American history , while on the Vietnamese side, the personalities from both the North and the South of the country shaped the conflict. The weakness of leaders in the South and their treatment of their citizens often contrasted starkly with the North Vietnamese authorities, and contributed to the eventual collapse of the state.

The Americans

PRESIDENT EISENHO

President Eisenhower was born in Texas in 1890. He had a decorated military career, which included commanding the troops invading France on D-Day, 1944. As President he adopted a hard line towards Communism at home and abroad. He decided against helping France at Dienbienphu, however, having previously supported them. Eisenhower remained supportive of the Diem regime in South Vietnam, despite its unpopularity.

PRESIDENT KENNEDY

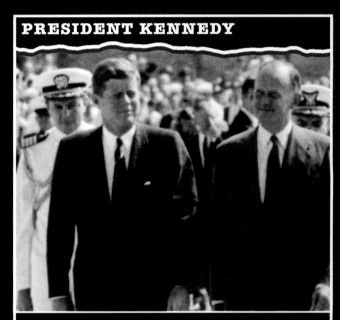

John F Kennedy was born in Brookline, Massachusetts, in 1917. He was a national war hero during the Second World War and went on to become the youngest ever president when elected in 1960. Kennedy resided over the Bay of Pigs failure and was a fierce opponent of Communism. In the 1960s, Kennedy decided that "Vietnam was the place" to halt the spread of Communism. He was assassinated in 1963.

PRESIDENT JOHNSON

Lyndon B Johnson was born in Texas in 1908. When President Kennedy was assassinated, Johnson became President. He took the United States deeper into Vietnam, with bombing of North Vietnam and troop deployment escalating dramatically under his presidency.

ROBERT MACNAMARA

Robert Macnamara was born in San Francisco in 1916. At the request of President-elect John F Kennedy, McNamara agreed to serve as Secretary of Defense of the United States, a position he held from 1961 until 1968.

PRESIDENT NIXON

Richard Nixon was born in California in 1913. He served in the Eisenhower administration and became president in 1968. Despite a promise to remove troops from Vietnam during the 1968 elections, a peace agreement was not signed until 1973.

Born in Germany in 1923, Kissinger came to the United States in 1938. He was appointed national security adviser by Nixon in 1969, and helped negotiate the Paris Agreement with Le Duc Tho in 1973. He helped improve relations with both China and the Soviet Union.

The South Vietnamese

PRESIDENT **DIEM**

Ngo Dinh Diem was born in Vietnam in 1901. After the Geneva conference in 1954, Diem became the new ruler of South Vietnam. After angering Buddhists with his draconian policies and violence, President Diem was overthrown by a military coup in November 1963.

PRESIDENT **THIEU**

Nguyen Van Thieu was born on April 5, 1923, in Ninh Tvuan, central Vietnam. He served in the French-supported Vietnam National Army from 1948–1954, fighting the pro-Communist forces of Ho Chi Minh. He became South Vietnam's head of state under Prime Minister Ky's government between 1965 and 1967. On September 3, 1967, Thieu became South Vietnam's President, a position he held until the Communist victory in 1975.

The North Vietnamese

HO CHI MINH

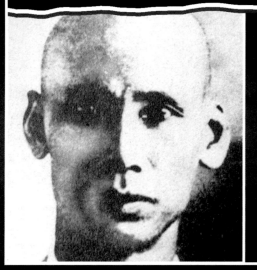

Nguyen That Thanh was born in 1890 in central Vietnam. He became a passionate supporter of the Communist cause while living in Europe between 1915–1923. Thanh then moved to Hong Kong, where he founded the Vietnamese Communist Party. In 1941 Thanh created the Vietminh, and changed his name to Ho Chi Minh, which means "He Who Enlightens". He proclaimed Vietnam independent from France in 1945, and continued to fight the French, then the United States from 1954. Ho Chi Minh earned the nickname "Uncle Ho". This popular figure stayed president of North Vietnam until his death in 1969.

GENERAL **GIAP**

Born in 1911, Vo Nguyen Giap became one of the most important military figures in North Vietnam. Giap made the People's Army of Vietnam (PAVN) into a force that defeated the French at Dien Bien Phu in May 1954. In the fight against the United States, Giap was the architect of the Tet offensive. He retired in 1973 after the failed Easter Offensive. Giap was given the Gold Star Order, Vietnam's highest decorative honor in 1992.

PRESIDENT **LE DUAN**

Le Duan was born in 1907 in central Vietnam. He joined the Communist party as a young man, and by 1959 he was secretary general. Le Duan played a key role in the insurgency in South Vietnam. He was responsible for the creation of the People's Revolutionary Party in 1962, a key part of the National Liberation Front. Le Duan became leader of North Vietnam after Ho Chi Minh's death in 1969.

LE DUC THO

Le Duc Tho was born in North Vietnam in 1911. Tho helped found the Indo-chinese Communist Party in 1930. In 1945 Tho established the Vietnam Revolutionary League (Vietminh) with Ho Chi Minh and Vo Nguyen Giap. Ten years of imprisonment by the French did not lessen his commitment to the Vietminh, Tho was in charge of the Vietminh until 1954, when he joined the the Communist Party of Vietnam. Tho continued to lead the insurgence in South Vietnam, while at the same time talking with Henry Kissinger with a view to a peace deal. Le Duc Tho rejected the Nobel Peace Prize awarded to himself and Kissinger jointly in 1973.

GLOSSARY

Agent Orange A spray containing a chemical called Dioxin which was used to kill vegetation over large areas of the Vietnamese jungle.

Allies In World War II, the Allies included the USA, Britain and the Commonwealth, the USSR and France who joined together to fight the Axis forces of Germany, Japan and Italy.

Amerasian Person of mixed American and Asian blood; usually the child of an Asian (especially Vietnamese) mother and an American (often a GI) father.

ARVN Army of the Republic of Vietnam, set up by Diem in North Vietnam to fight communists in South Vietnam.

Atom The smallest part of a particle. Atoms are also used as the source of nuclear energy.

Boat people Vietnamese refugees, mainly from the South, who fled the country after 1975 to escape persecution by the communist regime.

Buddhism A way of life followed by many Vietnamese people that strives for spiritual purity.

Capitalist A person who believes in the importance of individual rights and the ability of a person to create their own financial rewards, with minimal interference from governments.

CIDG Civilian Irregular Defence Groups, set up by the United States to provide surveillance in the mountains of Vietnam.

Cold War Hostile, but non-violent, relationship between the United States and the USSR and their respective Allies from the end of World War II to the 1980s.

Communist a person who believes that society should be classless, that private property should be abolished and that land and factories should be collectively owned and controlled.

Congress The federal legislature of the United States.

COSVN The Vietnamese Communist office in Cambodia.

Democrat a person who believes in the type of government in which power belongs to the people, and is administered on their behalf by elected representatives.

Democratic A system of government where all of a country's population has a vote in choosing who runs that nation's government.

Guerrilla a member of a force that engages in warfare, especially the harassment of an army, usually operating in small groups.

ICP Indochinese Communist Party, set up in Hong Kong in 1929 by Ho Chi Minh.

Iron Curtain The term used to describe the dividing line in Europe between capitalist countries in the West and communist countries in the East.

Iron Triangle The name during the Vietnam War for an area northwest of Saigon.

Leap day An extra day (February 29) inserted in the calendar every four years, helping to keep the calendar in harmony with the rotation of the earth.

MIA Missing in Action, a name given to soldiers still unaccounted for after the end of the Vietnam war. A few Americans believe that soldiers are still being held prisoner in Vietnam.

Nationalist a person who favours or fights for the unity, independence and interests of a nation.

NATO North Atlantic Treaty Organization. A coalition of Western countries, including Britain, the USA, France and Canada, in response to the apparent threat from communist countries.

NLF National Liberation Front (Viet Cong) formed by communist supporters in South Vietnam in 1960 to organize resistance efforts.

NVA North Vietnamese Army, formed by Ho Chi Minh.

Peacekeeping Force A military force that is sent into a war-torn region in an attempt to keep the peace.

PLAF People's Liberation Armed Forces formed by communist supporters in South Vietnam in 1960 to run the military side of the conflict (see also NLF).

Propaganda The manipulation of information and news so that a particular political message can be conveyed.

Purple Heart A US medal awarded for wounds received on active service.

Republic A form of government without a monarch in which supreme power is vested in the people and their elected representatives.

Reunify Re-join a country that has been divided through war.

Russian A citizen of Russia, or of the former USSR.

SALT Strategic Arms Limitation Talks. These were a series of meetings between the political leaders of the USA and USSR in which the limiting of nuclear weapons was discussed and some agreements were made.

SDI Strategic Defence Initiative. Popularly known as 'Star Wars', this was a high-tech defence system developed by the USA that was designed to destroy incoming Soviet nuclear missiles should a nuclear war ever begin.

SEATO South East Asia Treaty Organisation, set up between the United States and a number of countries to protect Vietnam from aggression.

Soviet The name of a council in a communist country, or somebody or something from a communist country.

Soviet Bloc Name given to the communist countries of Eastern Europe (also known as the Eastern Bloc).

Tet Important public holiday in Vietnam.

USSR Union of Soviet Socialist Republics. Enormous communist country including Russia, Latvia, the Ukraine and Georgia. It broke up in 1991 when the Communist Party lost power.

Vietminh Vietnamese nationalist organisation set up by Ho Chi Minh.

Warsaw Pact Coalition of former communist countries, including the USSR, Poland, East Germany and Czechoslovakia, in response to the foundation of NATO by Western countries.

INDEX

M

McNamara, Robert 21, 25, 41
Maddox 14
"missing in action" (*MIA*)
    37, 38
music 32
My Lai 22–23

National Liberation Front
    (*NLF*) (*Viet Cong*)
American search and destroy
    missions 18–19, 22–23
    escalation of conflict 15–16
    formation 11–12
New Zealand 16
Nixon, President Richard
    24–25, 27, 28, 41
NLF see *National Liberation*
    Front
North Vietnam
    division of Vietnam 4, 10–11
    talks with United States 24,
    26–27
    war with South Vietnam
    11–16, 17–19, 23–29
North Vietnamese Army
    (*NVA*) 11–12, 17, 28–29
NVA see *North Vietnamese*
    Army

P

Paris Peace Accords 1973
    26–27
peace talks 24, 26–27
Pentagon Papers 25
People's Liberation Armed
    Forces (*PLAF*) 11–12
PLAF *see People's Liberation*
Armed Forces

Platoon 30
Pleku 15
popular culture 30–33
prisoners of war 27–28

R

Rolling Thunder,
    Operation 15, 16, 20
Roosevelt, President
    Franklin Delano 10

S

Saigon 5, 28–29
search and destroy 18–19
SEATO see *South East Asia*
    Treaty Organisation
soldiers
    artists 32–33
    draft 21–22
    life in Vietnam 16–17
    "missing in action" (*MIA*)
    37, 38
    My Lai 22–23
    return to civilian life 6, 7
    war memorial 36–37
South East Asia Treaty
Organisation (*SEATO*) 11
South Korea 16
South Vietnam
    communist regime 35–36
    division of Vietnam 4, 10–11
    war with North Vietnam
    11–16, 17–19, 23–29
strategic hamlets 12–13
Struggle Movement 19

T

teach-ins 25
Tet Offensive 23–24
Thich Quang Duc 13

Thieu, President
    Nguyen Van 16, 27, 28, 42
Turner Joy 14

U

United States
    effect of Vietnam War 6,
    36–39
    post-war relations with
    Vietnam 38–39
    support for South Vietnam 5,
    11–13, 15–16
    trade embargo on Vietnam
    6, 38
    war with North Vietnam
    14–29

V

Viet Cong see *National*
    Liberation Front
Vietminh 10
Vietnam 4
    after the war 5–6, 7,
    34–36, 38
    American trade embargo
    6, 38
    division of 4, 10–11
    invasion of Cambodia
    34–35, 38
    post-war relations with the
    United States 38–39
    tourism 38
    see also *North Vietnam;*
    South Vietnam
Vietnamization 24–25

W

Westmoreland, General
    William Childs 17, 18, 25
World War II 9–10

47

ACKNOWLEDGEMENTS

PICTURE CREDITS:

Every effort has been made to trace the copyright holders, and we apologize in advance for any unintentional ommissions. We would be pleased to insert the appropriate acknowledgements in any subsequent edition of this publication.

B=bottom; C=centre; L=left; R=right; T=top

Corbis: 2 & 23b, 4-5, 7 all, 8-9c, 14b, 15t, 16b, 20b, 20t, 26b, 27t, 28b, 29t, 34-35, 37b, 38-39 all. Everett Collection: 30l, 31t. Getty Images: 6t, 12b, 13b, 22t, 25b, Magnum Photos: 9b.